Ed Sheeran

ISBN 978-1-4950-0197-0

HAL•LEONARD® CORPORATION

7777 W. BLUEMOUND RD. P.O. BOX 13819 MILWAUKEE, WI 53213

Visit Hal Leonard Online at
www.halleonard.com

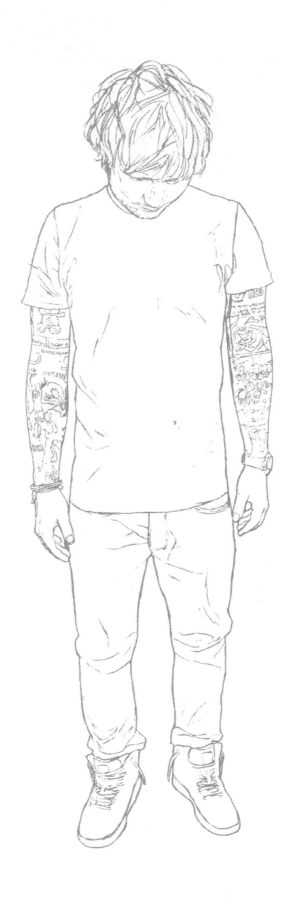

ONE

Words and Music by
ED SHEERAN

Bm   G   D

at all___ to leave.___   Would you take_
we see___ this through.___   We could stay_

A   G

a - way___ my hopes and dreams___ and just stay_
with - in___ these walls and bleed___ or just stay_

Em   G   A

with me._____ Ooh._____
with me._____ Oh,___ Lord___ now.

%⟍ D   F♯m/C♯

All my sen - ses come to life___ while I'm stum - bling home as

I'M A MESS

Words and Music by
ED SHEERAN

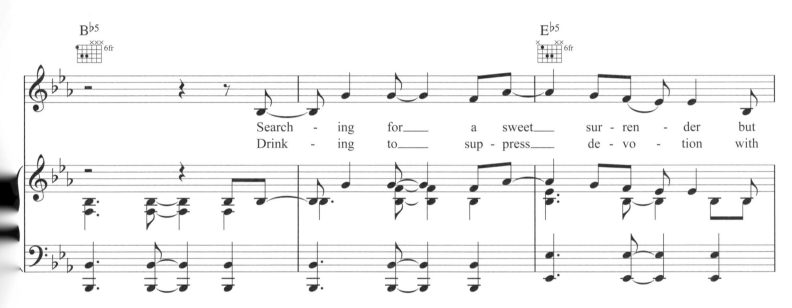

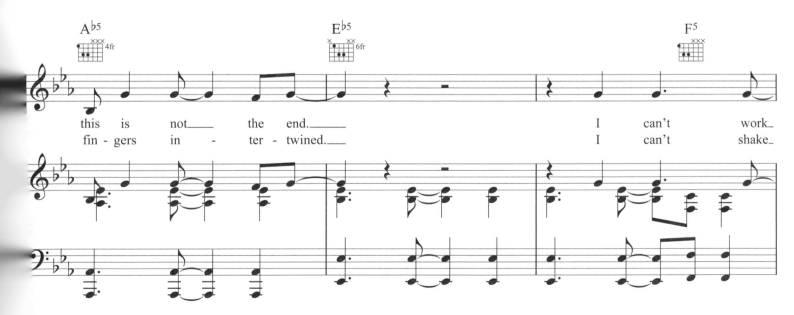

it out,___ how._____ Going through the mo-
this feel-ing now._____ We're go-ing through the mo-

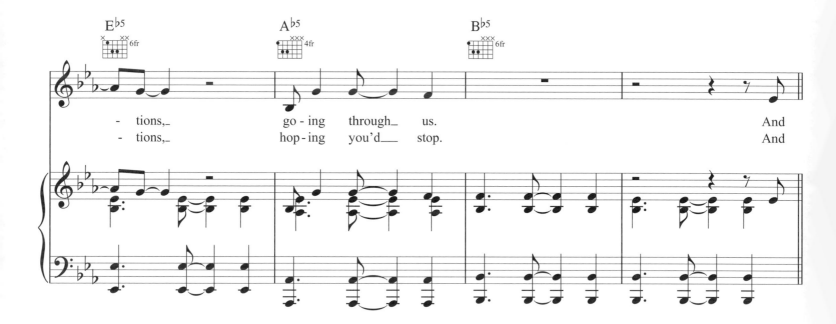

- tions,_ go-ing through_ us. And
- tions,_ hop-ing you'd__ stop. And

oh I've_____ known__ it for the long-est time,__ and all of my hopes,
oh I've_____ on - ly caused you pain__ I know,__ but all of my words

all of my own words___ are all___ o - ver writ-ten on___ the signs,___
will al - ways be - low._____ Of all,_____ all the love___ we spoke___

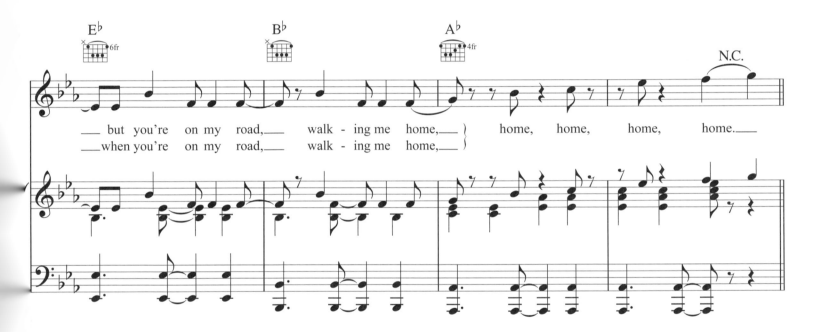

___ but you're on my road,___ walk - ing me home,___ home, home, home, home.___
___when you're on my road,___ walk - ing me home,___

See___ the flames___ in - side my eyes._____ It burns so

for how__ long,__ I love,_____ my__ lov - er.__ Now, now.

For how__ long,__ I love,_____ my__ lov - er?__ Now, now.

For how__ long,__ long I love,_____ my__ lov - er. Now, now.

For how__ long,__ long I love,_____ my__ lov - er.__ Now, now.

SING

Words and Music by ED SHEERAN
and PHARRELL WILLIAMS

G#m

we could get___ down,___ now.___ I don't wan - na know

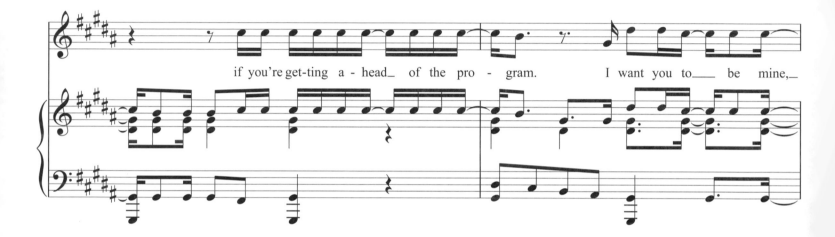

if you're get-ting a - head___ of the pro - gram. I want you to___ be mine,___

___ la - dy,___ and to hold your bod - y close. Take an-oth-er step in-to the no___

___man's land, for the long - est time,___ la - dy.___ I

need you darl - ing come on, set the tone.__ If you feel you're fall - ing, won't you let me know?__ Oh, oh,__

ooh.__ Oh, oh,__ ooh.__

If you love__ me come on, get in - volved__ feel it rush - ing through__ you from your head to toe.__ Oh, oh,__

ooh.__ Oh, oh,__ ooh.__ Sing!

I al-rea-dy know that she's a keep-er. Just from this one small act of kind-ness. I'm in

C#m

deep if an-y-bod-y finds out. I'm meant___ to drive home but I've drunk all of it now. Not

D.S. al Coda

so-ber-ing up, we just sit on the couch.___ One thing___ led to an-oth-er now she's kiss-ing my mouth.___ I

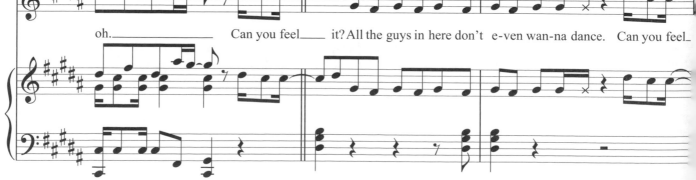

Coda

C#m

G#m

oh._____ Can you feel___ it? All the guys in here don't e-ven wan-na dance. Can you feel___

_____ it? All that I can hear is mu - sic from the back. Can you feel___ it?Found you hid-ing here so

won't you take my hand,___ darl - ing, un - til the beat kicks in a - gain. Can you feel___

___ it? *Vocal ad lib.*

Sing! I

need you darl - ing, come on set the tone._ If you feel you're fall-ing, won't you let me know. Oh, oh,_

ooh._ Oh, oh,_ ooh._ Sing!

If you love_me come on, get in-volved,_ feel it rush-ing through_you from your head to toe._Oh, oh,_

ooh._ Oh, oh,_ ooh._ Sing!

DON'T

Words and Music by ED SHEERAN,
DAWN ROBINSON, BEN LEVIN,
RAPHAEL SAADIQ, ALI JONES-MUHAMMAD
and CONESHA OWENS

met this girl___ late last___ year. She said don't you wor-ry if I dis-ap-pear.___ I told her
(2.) weeks I on-ly want to see___ her. We drink a-way the days with a take a-way___ piz-za.___ Be-fore, a text mes-

(Verse 3 see block lyrics)

-way for months un - til_____ our paths_crossed a - gain._____ She told me
Those shows have nev - er been what it's a - bout. But may - be we'll go to - geth - er and just fig -ure it out. I'd

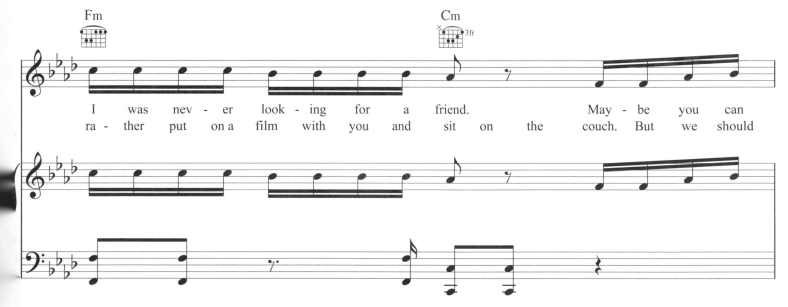

I was nev - er look - ing for a friend. May - be you can
ra - ther put on a film with you and sit on the couch. But we should

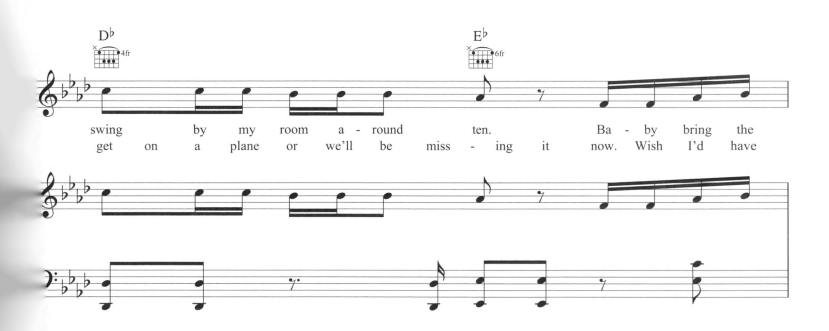

swing by my room a - round ten. Ba - by bring the
get on a plane or we'll be miss - ing it now. Wish I'd have

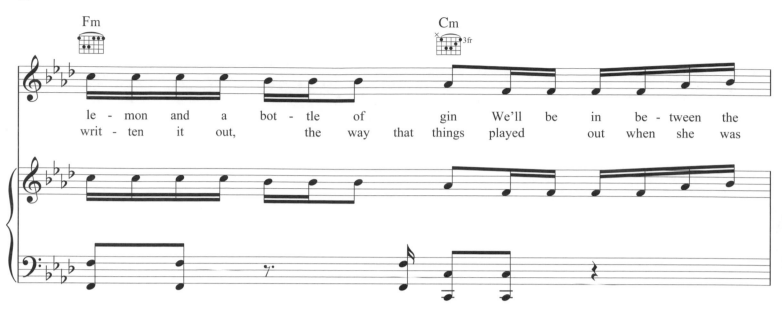

le - mon and a bot - tle of gin We'll be in be - tween the
writ - ten it out, the way that things played out when she was

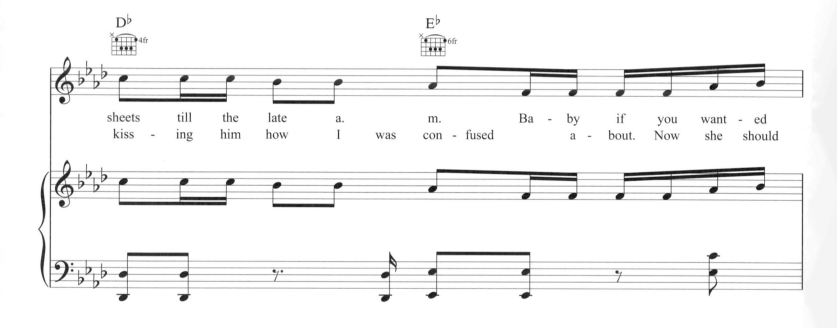

sheets till the late a. m. Ba - by if you want - ed
kiss - ing him how I was con - fused a - bout. Now she should

me then you should -'ve just said. She's sing - ing: Ah, la - ah - la - la.
fi - gure it out while I'm sat here sing - ing': Don't **** with my

love.   I told her, she   knows.   Take aim and re -

- load._____   I don't wan - na know that___ babe.   Ah,   la - ah - la - la.

Verse 3:

[Knock, knock, knock] on my hotel door.
I don't even know if she knows what for.
She was crying on my shoulder.
I already told ya.
Trust and respect is what we do this for.
I never intended to be next.
But you didn't need to take him to bed, that's all.
And I never saw him as a threat.
Until you disappeared with him to have sex, of course.
It's not like we were both on tour.
We were staying on the same ****ing hotel floor.
And I wasn't looking for a promise to commitment.
But it was never just fun and I thought you were different.
This is not the way you realise what you wanted.
It's a bit too much too late if I'm honest.
All this time, god knows, I'm singin':

NINA

Words and Music by ED SHEERAN,
JERMAINE SCOTT, ISRA ANDJA-DIUMI LOHATA,
JOHN McDAID and JAY LEE ROBERT HIPPOLYTE

Sing that song,__ go oh,__ won't you leave me now.__

claps   *claps*   *claps*

N.C.

Peo - ple grow__ and fall__ a - part__ but you can mend__ your bro - ken heart,__

claps   *claps*   *claps*   *claps*

take it back,__ go, oh,__ won't you leave me now. Ooh.....__

F#m   C#m   D

Oh,__ Ni - na, you should go,__ Ni - na. 'Cause I ain't ev - er com - ing
(vocal ad lib.)

PHOTOGRAPH

Words and Music by ED SHEERAN
and JOHN McDAID

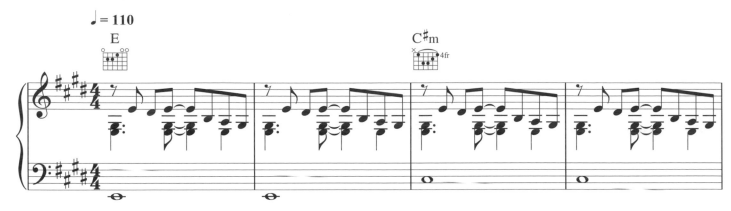

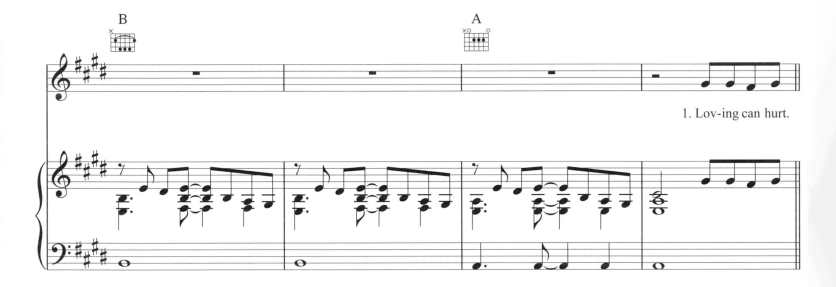

1. Lov-ing can hurt.

Lov-ing can hurt_____ some-times.
(2.) Lov-ing can mend_____ your soul.

But it's the on -
And is the on -

L.H. 2° only

BLOODSTREAM

Words and Music by ED SHEERAN,
AMIR IZADKHAH, KESI DRYDEN,
PIERS AGGETT, JOHN McDAID
and GARY LIGHTBODY

1. I've been spin-ning now_ for time, coup - le wom-en by__ my side.
2. I've been look-ing for a lov-er, thought I'd find her in a bot-tle.

I got sin-ning on my mind,_____ sip-ping on red wine.
God make me an - oth-er one.__ I'll be feel-ing this to-mor-row.

I've been sit-ting here_ for a - ges,__ rip-ping out__ the
Lord, for-give me for__ the things I've done.__ I was nev-er meant

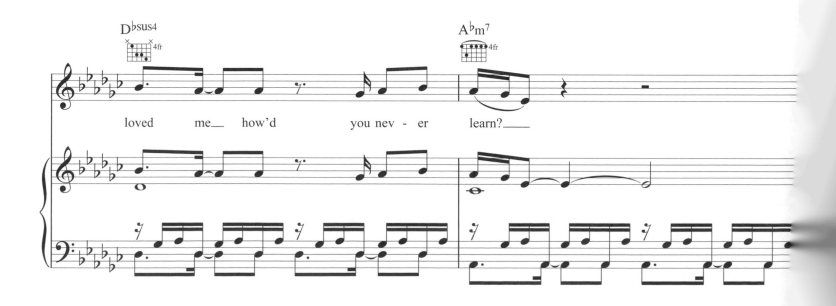

Fad-ing out a-gain, I____ feel the chem-i-cals burn

in my blood___ stream. So tell me when it kicks in.

Mm, mm,____ mm, mm,_____

mm, mm.___ Well, tell me when it kicks in.

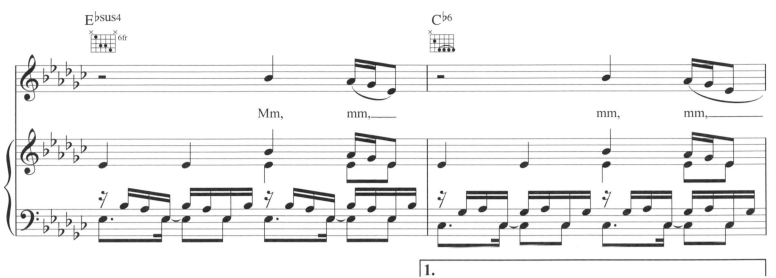

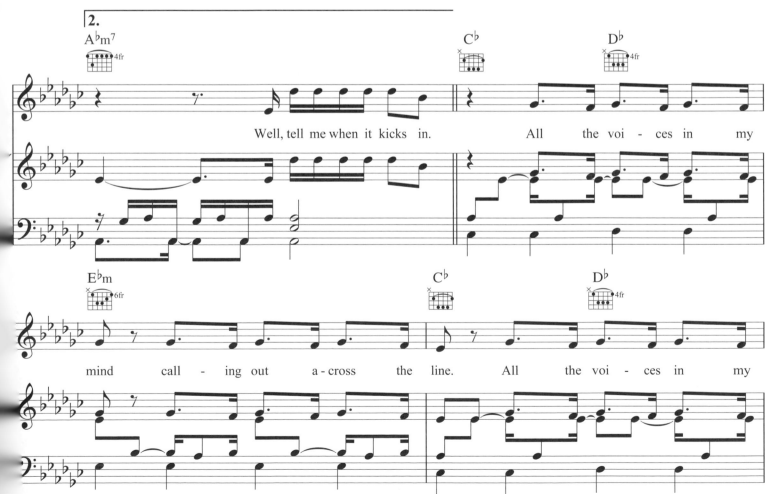

50

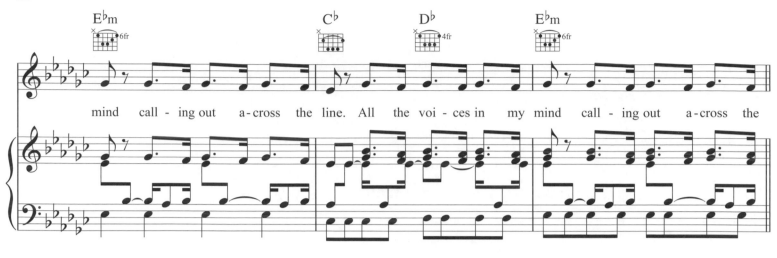

mind call - ing out a-cross the line. All the voi-ces in my mind call - ing out a-cross the

line. All the voi - ces in my mind call - ing out a-cross the

vocal ad lib.

Play 5 times

line. All the voi - ces in my mind call - ing out a-cross the

line. All the voi - ces in my mind... Bro - ken -

TENERIFE SEA

Words and Music by ED SHEERAN,
JOHN McDAID and FOY VANCE

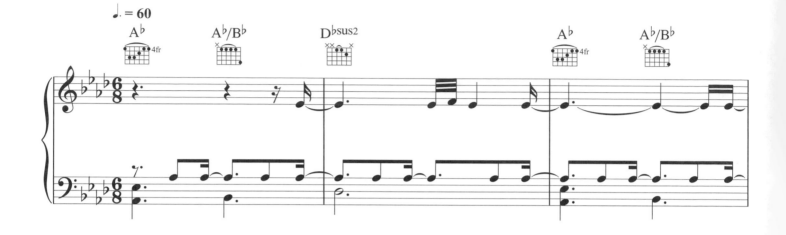

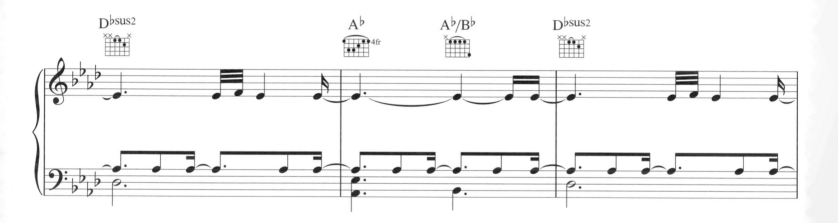

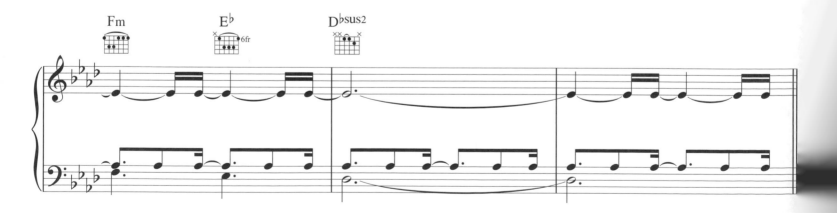

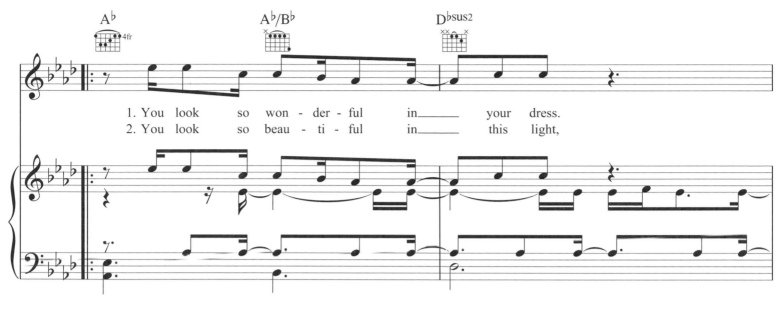

1. You look so won-der-ful in_____ your dress.
2. You look so beau-ti-ful in_____ this light,

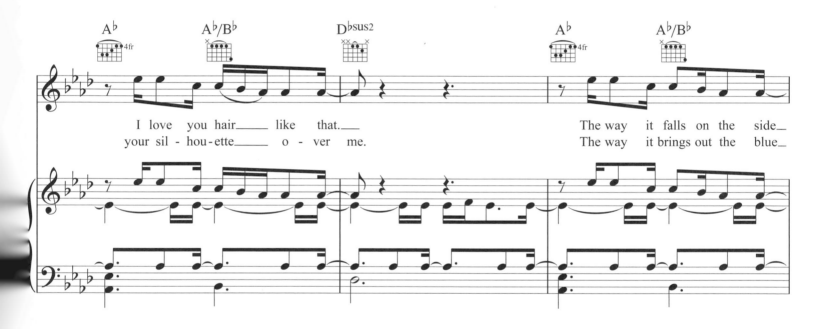

I love you hair_____ like that.__
your sil-hou-ette_____ o-ver me.

The way it falls on the side_
The way it brings out the blue_

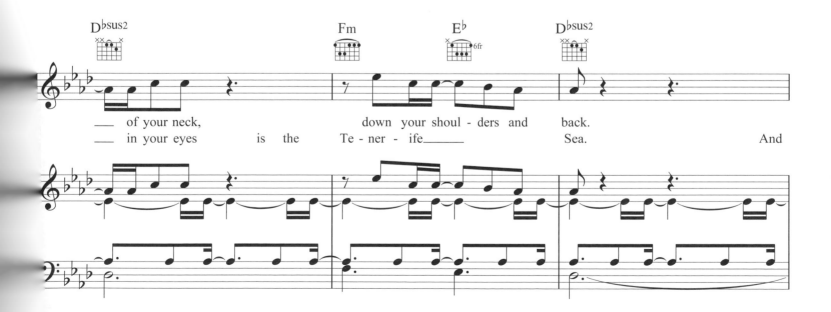

__ of your neck, down your shoul-ders and back.
__ in your eyes is the Te-ner-ife_____ Sea. And

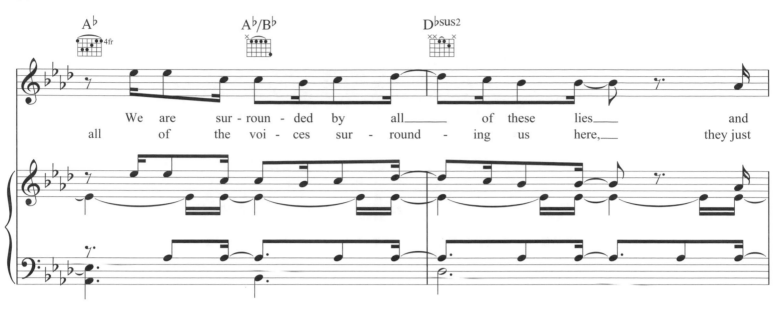

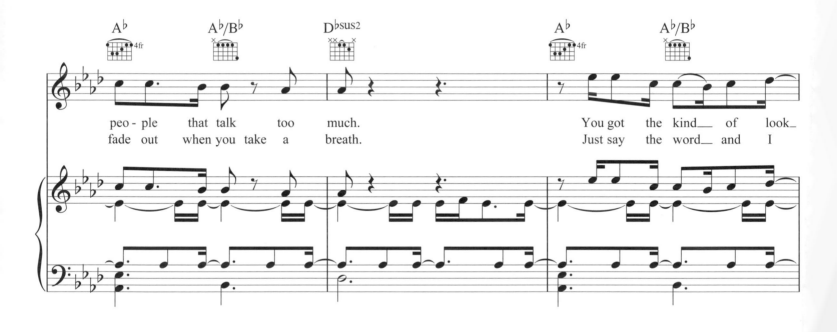

Should this be__ the last thing I see, I want you to know__ it's e-nough__ for me. 'Cause

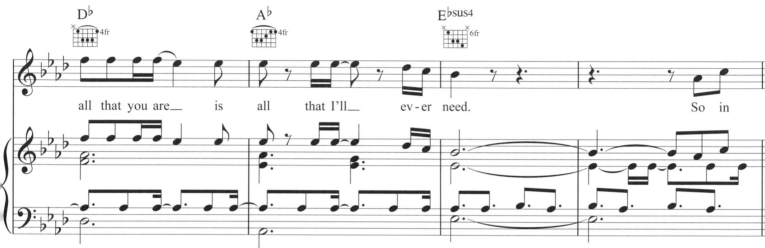

all that you are__ is all that I'll__ ev-er need. So in

love, so in love, so in

To Coda

love, so in love.

RUNAWAY

Words and Music by ED SHEERAN
and PHARRELL WILLIAMS

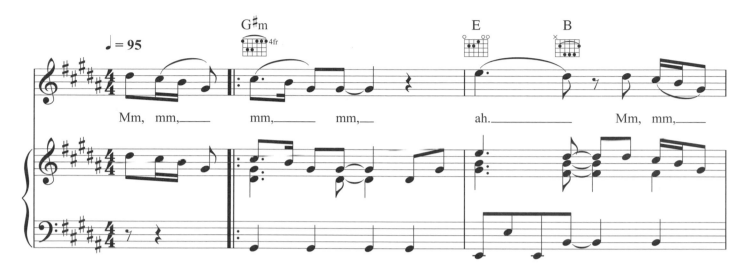

1. I've known it for a long time;___ dad-dy wakes to for a drink at nine.
2. I've nev-er seen my dad cry;___ cold___ as stone in the kit-chen light.

Dis - ap - pear - ing all night,___ I don't wan - na know where he's been ly - ing.
I tell you, it's a - bout time,___ but I was raised to keep___ qui - et.

I know what I wan - na do;___ wan - na run a - way, run a - way with you.
This is what I'm gon - na do;___ gon - na run a - way, gon - na make that move.

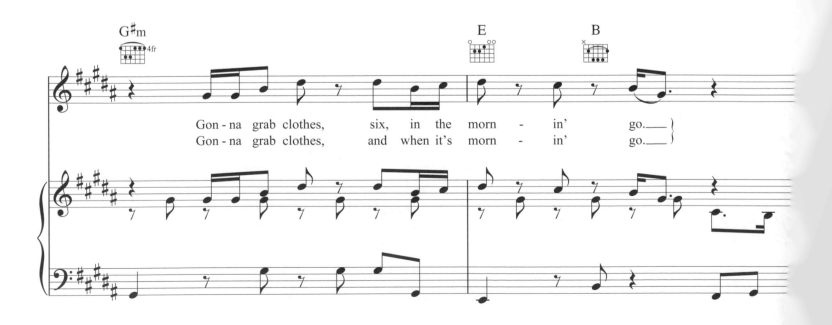

Gon - na grab clothes, six, in the morn - in' go.___ }
Gon - na grab clothes, and when it's morn - in' go.___ }

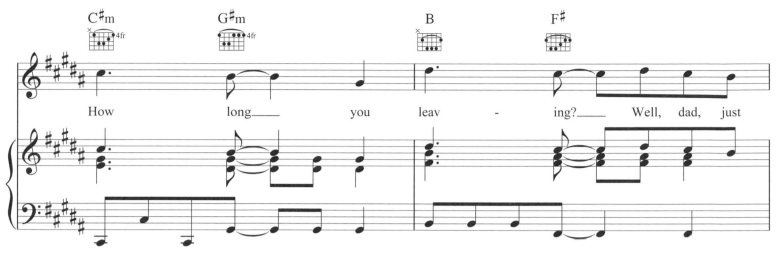

How long____ you leav - ing?____ Well, dad, just

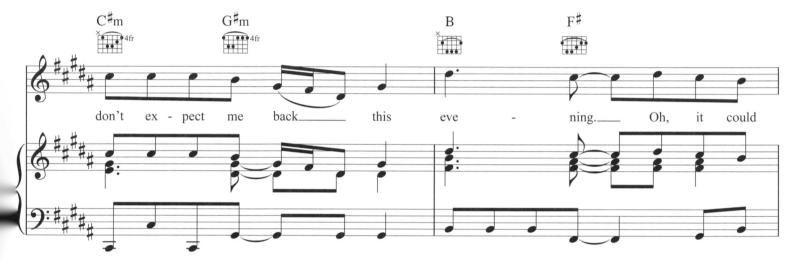

don't ex - pect me back____ this eve - ning.____ Oh, it could

take a bit of time to heal____ this.____ It's been a long____

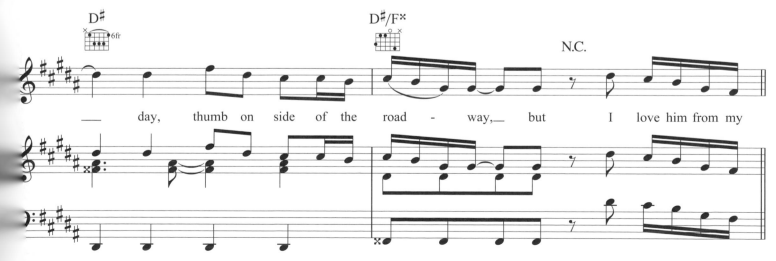

____ day, thumb on side of the road - way,____ but I love him from my

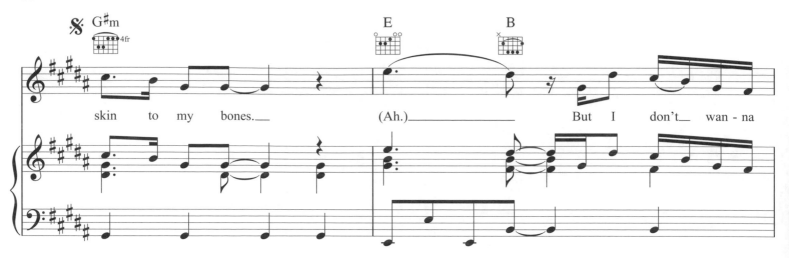

skin to my bones.___ (Ah.)_____ But I don't__ wan - na

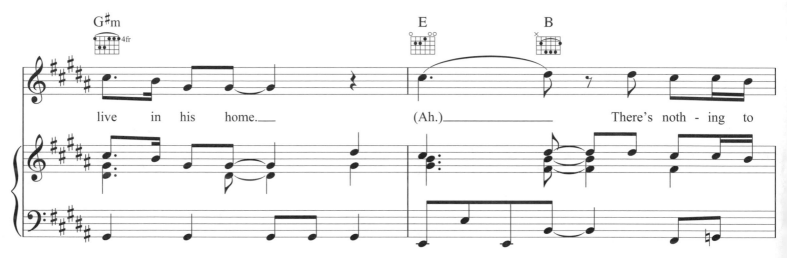

live in his home.___ (Ah.)_____ There's noth - ing to

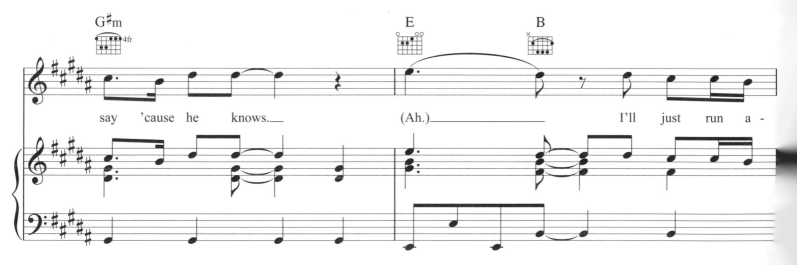

say 'cause he knows.___ (Ah.)_____ I'll just run a -

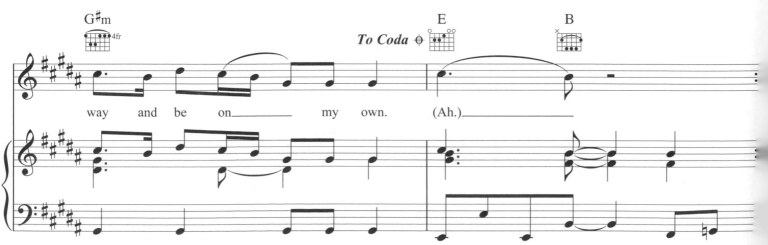

way and be on___ my own. (Ah.)_____

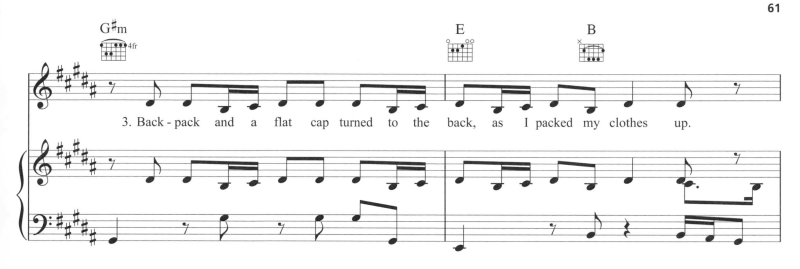

3. Back-pack and a flat cap turned to the back, as I packed my clothes up.

My dad was-n't down with that plan to at-tack, in-tends to show love.

I don't wan-na live this way. Gon-na take my things and go, but

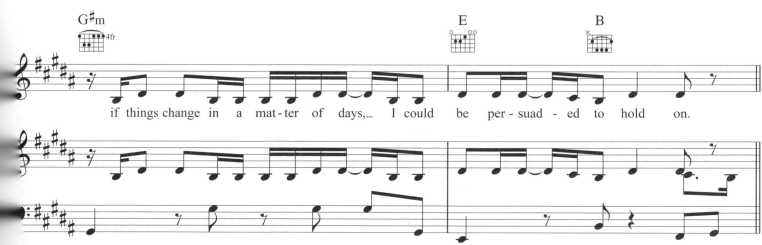

if things change in a mat-ter of days,_ I could be per-suad-ed to hold on.

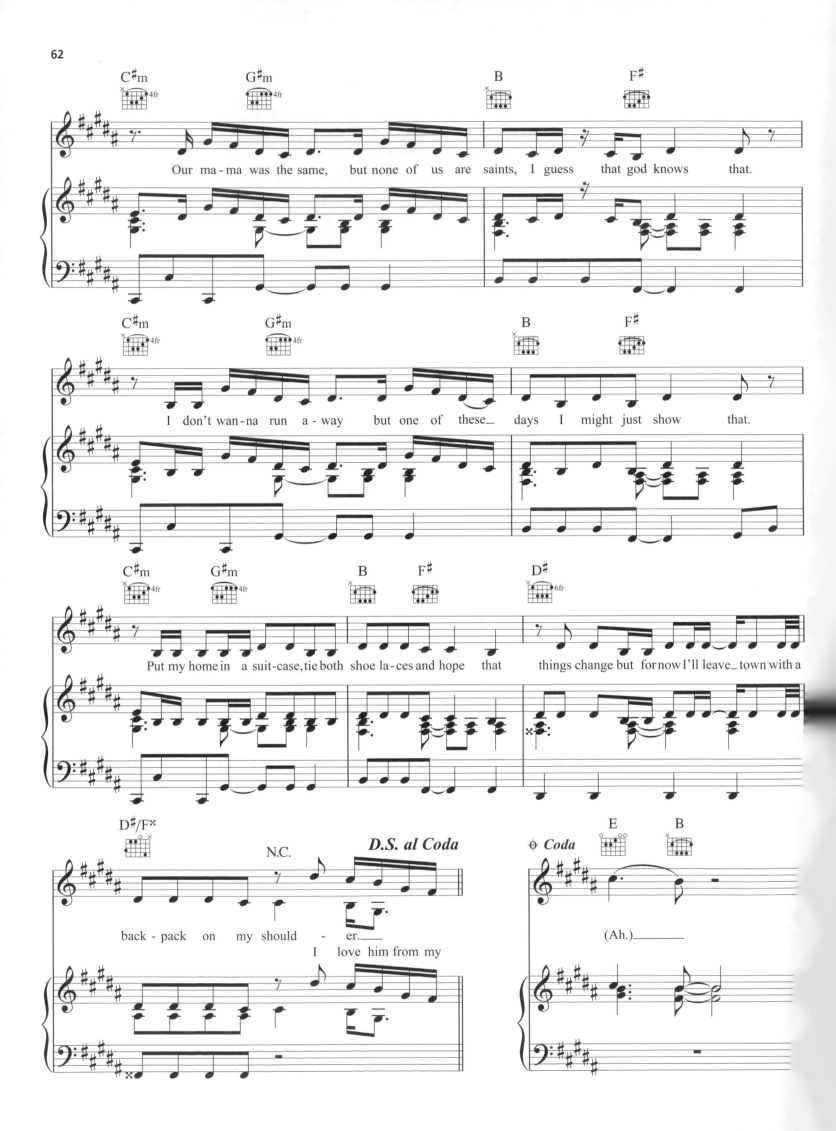

THE MAN

Words and Music by
ED SHEERAN

1. *Now, I don't wanna hate you,*

just wish you'd never gone for the man and waited two weeks at least before you let him take you, I stayed true
(2.) *tend to zone out up in my headphone to "Holocene". You promised your body but I'm away so much, I stay more celibate than in a*
(Verse 3 see block lyrics)

I kinda knew you liked the dude from private school, he's waiting for the time to move I knew he had his eyes on you.
monastery. I'm not cut out for life on the road, 'cause I didn't know I'd miss you this much and at the time we'd just go,

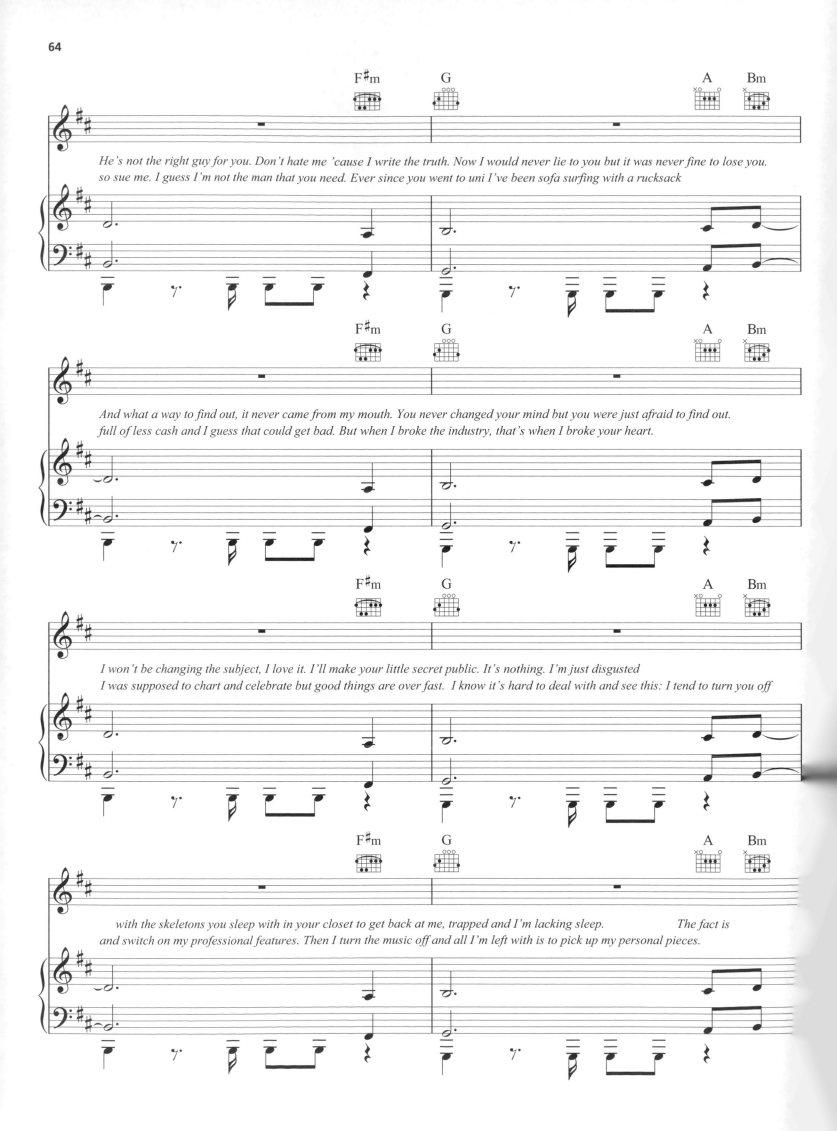

He's not the right guy for you. Don't hate me 'cause I write the truth. Now I would never lie to you but it was never fine to lose you.
so sue me. I guess I'm not the man that you need. Ever since you went to uni I've been sofa surfing with a rucksack

And what a way to find out, it never came from my mouth. You never changed your mind but you were just afraid to find out.
full of less cash and I guess that could get bad. But when I broke the industry, that's when I broke your heart.

I won't be changing the subject, I love it. I'll make your little secret public. It's nothing. I'm just disgusted
I was supposed to chart and celebrate but good things are over fast. I know it's hard to deal with and see this: I tend to turn you off

with the skeletons you sleep with in your closet to get back at me, trapped and I'm lacking sleep.   The fact is
and switch on my professional features. Then I turn the music off and all I'm left with is to pick up my personal pieces.

Verse 3:

Since you left I've given up my days off.
It's what I need to stay strong.
I know you have a day job but mine is 24/7.
I feel like writing a book, I guess I lied in the hook.
'Cause I still love you and I need you by my side if I could.
The irony is if my career and music didn't exist,
In six years, yeah, you'd probably be my wife with a kid.
I'm frightened to think if I depend on cider and drink
And lighting a spliff, I fall into a spiral and it's just hiding my
Misguiding thoughts that I'm trying to kill.
And I'd be writing my will before I'm 27.
I'll die from a thrill, go down in history as just a wasted talent.
Can I face the challenge or did I make a mistake erasing?
It's only therapy, my thoughts just get ahead of me.
Eventually I'll be fine, I know that it was never meant to be.
Either way I guess, I'm not prepared. But I'll say this:
These things happen for a reason and you can't change.
Take my apology. I'm sorry for the honesty, but I had to get this off my chest.

THINKING OUT LOUD

Words and Music by ED SHEERAN
and AMY WADGE

will be lov-ing you till__ we're se-ven-ty.__ And ba-by, my
soul could nev-er grow old,__ it's ev-er-green.__ And ba-by, your

heart could still feel as hard__ at twen-ty-three._____ And I'm think-ing 'bout how__
smile's for-ev-er in my mind__ and mem-o-ry._____ And I'm think-ing 'bout how__

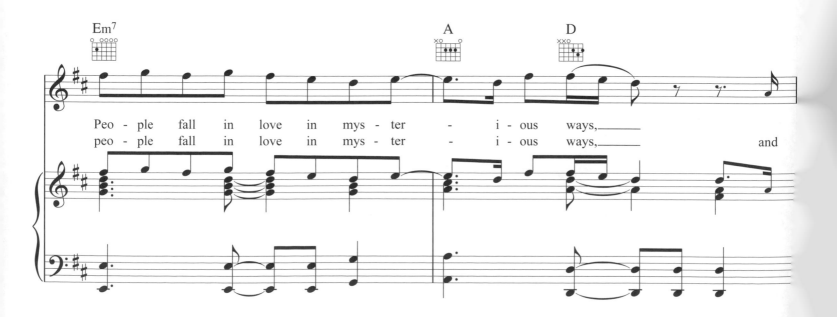

Peo-ple fall in love in mys-ter - i-ous ways,__
peo-ple fall in love in mys-ter - i-ous ways,__ and

may - be just the touch of a hand.___ Well me I fall in love with you ev -
may - be it's all part of a plan.___ Well I'll just keep on mak - ing the same___

- ry sin - gle day.___ And I just wan - na tell you I am.___ So hon - ey now,___
___ mis - takes,___ hop - ing that you'll un - der - stand.___ That ba - by now,___

take me in - to your lov - ing arms.___

la, la, la, la, la, la, la, la, la, la.)

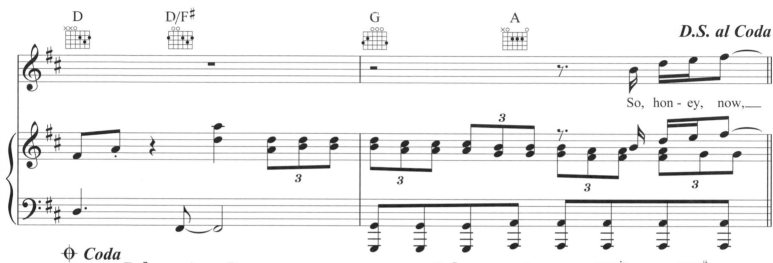

D.S. al Coda

So, hon - ey, now,___

⊕ Coda

where we are. Ba - by, we found love right

where we are.___ And we found love right where we are.___

AFIRE LOVE

Words and Music by ED SHEERAN,
JOHN McDAID, CHRISTOPHE BECK
and FOY VANCE

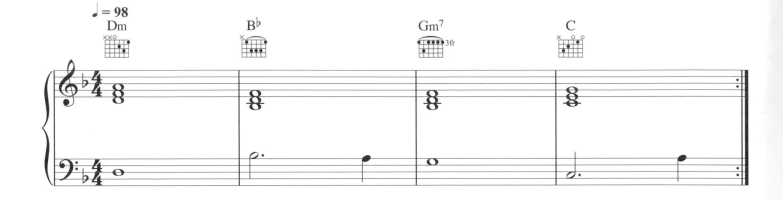

1. Things were all good yes - ter - day___ and then the dev - il took your mem - o - ry.

2. Things were all good yes - ter - day___ and then the dev - il took your breath a - way.

And you're not the on - ly one.___ Al-though my

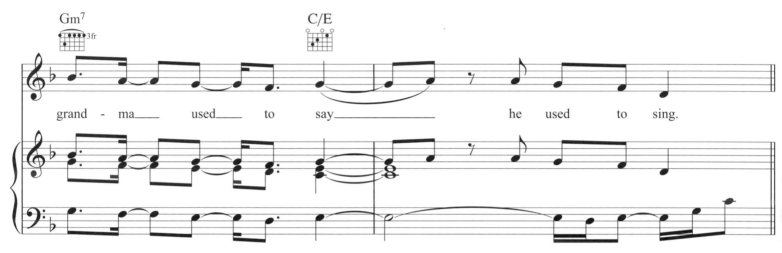

grand - ma___ used___ to say_____ he used to sing.

Darl - ing, hold in my your arms the way you did last___ night. And we'll lie___ in - side,___

___ a lit-tle while here, oh._____ I could look in-to your eyes un-til the sun comes_ up.

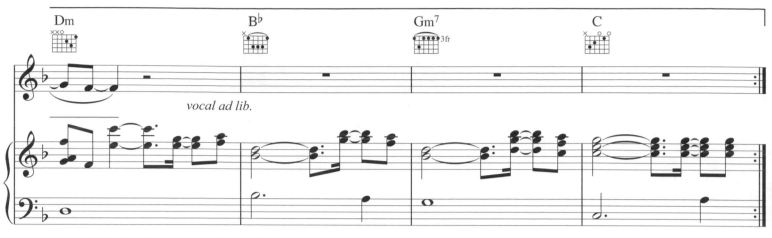

TAKE IT BACK

Words and Music by ED SHEERAN
and JOHN McDAID

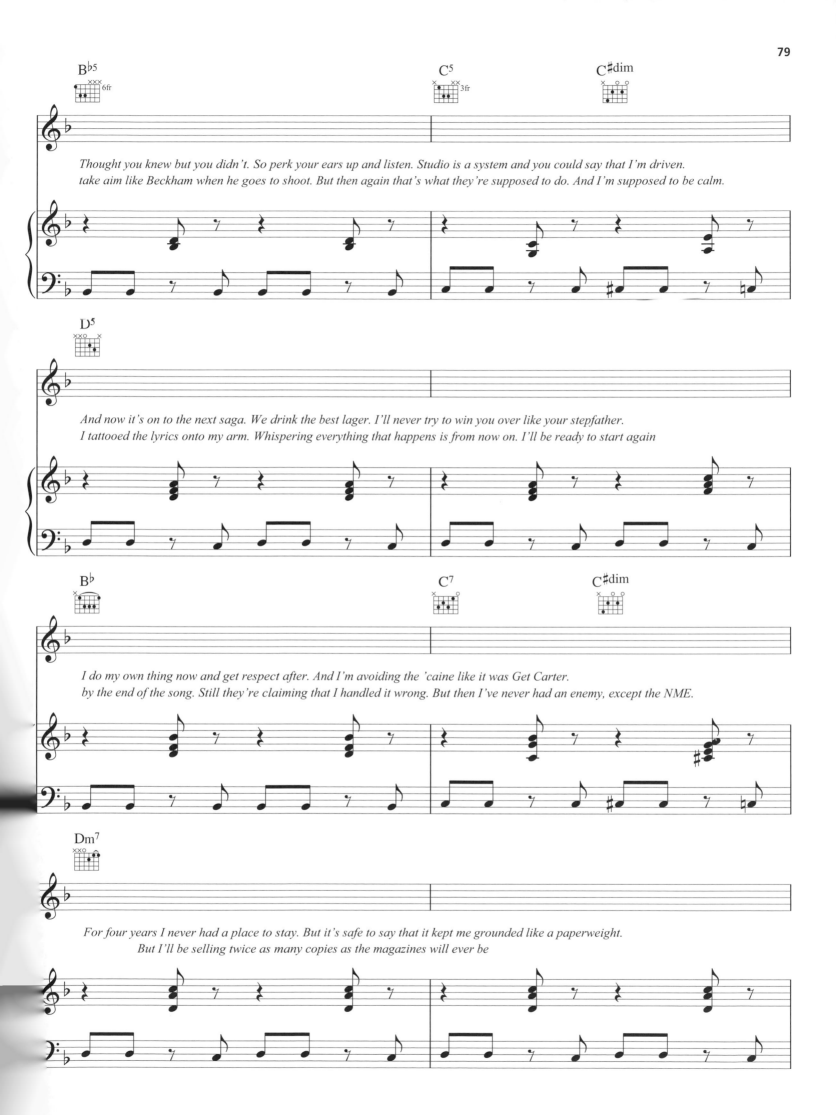

B♭5

C5

C♯dim

Thought you knew but you didn't. So perk your ears up and listen. Studio is a system and you could say that I'm driven.
take aim like Beckham when he goes to shoot. But then again that's what they're supposed to do. And I'm supposed to be calm.

D5

And now it's on to the next saga. We drink the best lager. I'll never try to win you over like your stepfather.
I tattooed the lyrics onto my arm. Whispering everything that happens is from now on. I'll be ready to start again

B♭

C7

C♯dim

I do my own thing now and get respect after. And I'm avoiding the 'caine like it was Get Carter.
by the end of the song. Still they're claiming that I handled it wrong. But then I've never had an enemy, except the NME.

Dm7

For four years I never had a place to stay. But it's safe to say that it kept me grounded like a paperweight.
But I'll be selling twice as many copies as the magazines will ever be

on and take it back for us._____ Don't you fade in-to the back, love.

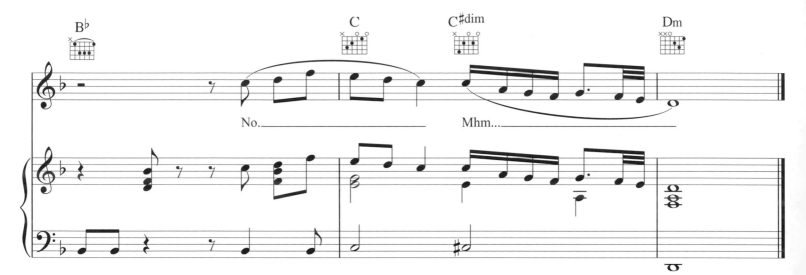

No._____ Mhm..._____

Verse 3:

And take it back now.
Now, I don't ever wanna be perfect.
'Cause I'm a singer that you never wanna see shirtless.
And I accept the fact that someone's got to win worst-dressed.
Taken my first steps into the scene, giving me focus.
Putting on a brave face, like Timothy Dalton.
Considering a name change, thinking it was hopeless.
Rhyming over recordings, avoiding tradition.
'Cause every day's a lyric and the melody can be written.
Now absence can make your heart ache,
But drinking absinthe can change your mind-state, vividly.
Need to let my liver be. And I'll say it again:
Living life on the edge with a close handful of friends
It's good advice from the man that took his life on the road with me.
And I hope to see him blowing up globally
'Cause that's how it's supposed to be. I'm screaming out vocally.
It might seem totally impossible, achieving life's dreams.
But I just write schemes.
I'm never having a stylist, giving me tight jeans.
Madison Square Garden is where I might be.
But more likely you find me in the back room of a dive bar with my mates.
Having a pint of McDaid discussing records we made.
And every single second knowing that we'll never betray the way we were raised,
Remembering our background, sat down.
That's how we plan it out. It's time to take it back now.

SHIRTSLEEVES

Words and Music by
ED SHEERAN

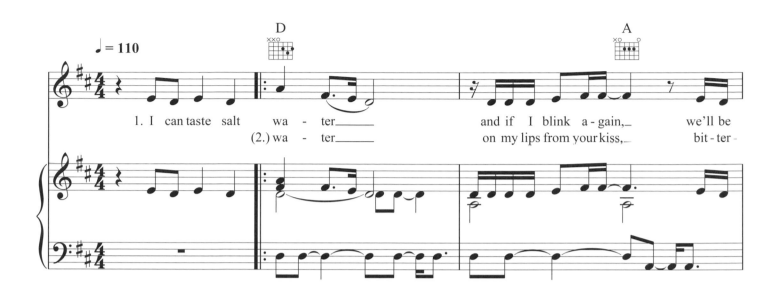

1. I can taste salt wa - ter_____ and if I blink a - gain,_ we'll be
(2.) wa - ter_____ on my lips from your kiss, bit - ter -

sink - ing in._ So we'll learn to swim in the o - ceans you made._
- ness._ And I'll drown with - in the_ o - ceans you made._

_ I'll hold_ ya_ and you'll think of him._
_ And I hate to love you. These cuffs are cov - ered in your make - up.

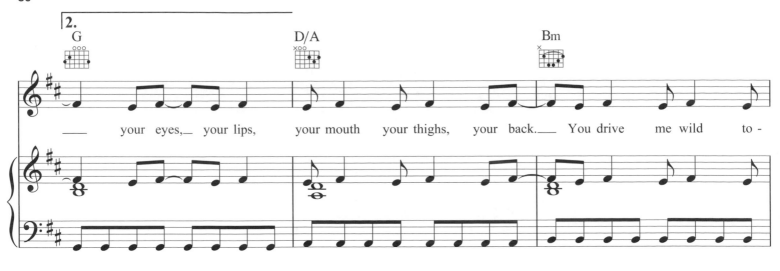

your eyes,_ your lips, your mouth your thighs, your back.__ You drive me wild to-

-night. The fact__ is I'm_____ I'm on the way_ home,__ I'm on the way_ home.__

__ I lied, I tried to

cry but I'm,___ I'm drown-ing in___ the o - ceans you made.__

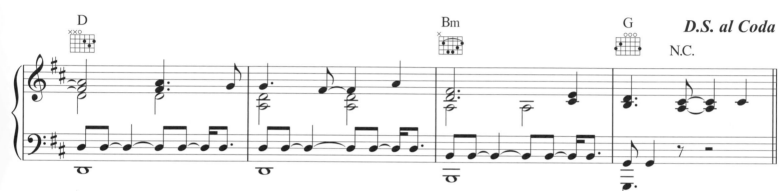

your eyes,_____ your eyes, your eyes, your eyes, your_____

_____ eyes._____

EVEN MY DAD DOES SOMETIMES

Words and Music by ED SHEERAN
and AMY WADGE

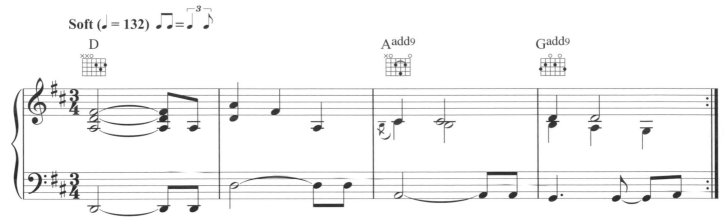

1. It's al - right to cry,_____ e - ven my dad__ does some -
2. It's al - right to shake,_____ e - ven my hand__ does some -

- times.
- times.

But just for to-night___ hold
But just for to-day___ hold

on.
on.

So live life like you're giv-ing up,___

'cause you act like you are.

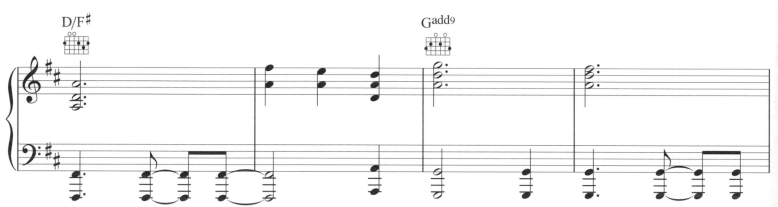

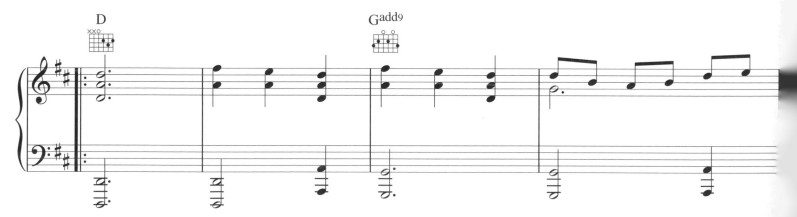

I SEE FIRE

from THE HOBBIT: THE DESOLATION OF SMAUG

Words and Music by
ED SHEERAN

* Melody sung in octaves throughout.   †Symbols in parentheses represent chord names with respect to capoed guitar.
Symbols above represent actual sounding chords.